The Heart and Other Stories

By
Grace Yan

Acknowledgement

"This book and its short stories wouldn't be possible without Ann, my very first creative writing tutor. Congrats on graduating college, and I wish you all the happiness in the world!"

Table of Contents

The Color Merchant

Everyone who lived underground knew the sky belonged to the rich. You could sell your soul, your house, your gold mine, and the souls of your mine workers and still not have enough for a ticket to the surface— if there was even a buyer in the first place.

Luckily, there were other ways to see the sky. Like stealing it.

The Color Merchant was, at best, a thief. At worst, a demon. In fact, one of the leading theories surrounding him is that he actually isn't human. How could he, when he carves little pieces out of the sky, package and sell underground? So, for the surface dwellers, the Color Merchant was a demon. Evil as that. For most undergrounders, he was a demon but a compassionate one. Others say he's just a bored, mischievous god. A very small minority maintains he's as human as everyone else.

However, none of the theories can explain how the Color Merchant gets places. He simply appears, popping up in a lonely corner of town square or a dark back alleyway. It's like he phases through the earth. Sometimes, he's a peddling merchant. Sometimes, he's a food vendor. Sometimes, he's a doctor.

"A doctor."

That's who Elijah met. The boy halted in his tracks and turned around. He hadn't thought much of it when the stranger first sat down next to him on the bench he was resting at. But now, as he was about to leave, Elijah could feel the skin tingling on his back.

"A doctor? Who?"

"Me. I'm a doctor."

Elijah scrutinized the man a second time. Medical practitioners were extremely rare in the Underground. Elijah envisioned most as

1

gray-haired, hunched, hook-nosed men scurrying about with strange concoctions. Now that he was looking closer, this stranger fit the archetype in a sense. He wore a long white coat and muddy leather boots. His face was sculpted by time, rain, and storm, carving valleys into his forehead and cheekbones. A pair of round spectacles hung at the sharp ridge of his nose and glinted with a dull sheen in the glow of a nearby street gas lamp. The man looked back at the boy with inscrutable eyes. They were a pair of eyes that had seen the blooming and withering of countless gardens.

Elijah's gaze drifted up, and he stared at the old man's blue helmet. He couldn't make sense of it. The color. It was so vibrant. It was the color of a cool updraft wind from the mines, free and deep. The color of his grandmother rising from her seat after a long day of work. The color of a promise.

Unconsciously, Elijah lifted a hand to feel the surface of his own helmet. It was already cratered and chipped from all the rocks that occasionally fall from the cave ceiling. He looked back at the man's helmet, which was smoother and shinier than the back of a freshly forged shovel. Strange.

"You aren't duping me?"

"You're too poor to dupe, boy."

Elijah's scabbed fingers tightened around the straps of his bag. They contained groceries from the market that he would have to bring home soon. The man before him looked rather well-off based on his clothes, so the likelihood of this whole incident being an elaborate set up for a robbery was pretty low. But you couldn't ever be too cautious, not Underground, at least.

"Well? Then how good are you?"

"I can cure anything in the world."

2

This sounded more and more like a scam. Elijah hadn't lived a decade and a half for nothing. He took a step back and glared at the man. "Liar."

"I really can."

"Prove it."

"I'll cure *you*." He raised a slender finger and pointed it straight at Elijah.

"Me? I'm not sick."

The man smiled. Almost like he was amused. Almost. "Everyone Underground is sick."

Underground. Was this a Surfacer? Elijah twisted his retort into a question. "Oh really? From what?"

The man's smile grew teeth. "Blindness."

He said it so convincingly, so charismatically, Elijah had to blink a couple times just to be sure that he really *wasn't* blind. "What are you talking about?"

The doctor suddenly took something out of his coat pocket. "The fact that you can't see that you're blind proves your blindness. Luckily for you," he held out the object towards Elijah, "I have just the prescription."

It was a small, circular glass jar no thicker or taller than the width of Elijah's thumb and capped with a thin, black lid. Inside the jar was a single, sight-searing color. Elijah stumbled forward like a starving man to a feast, all reservations forgotten, and picked the jar up with shaky fingers.

At first, he thought the item inside was a suspended, frozen candle flame. It was certainly the color of one. A kind of orange-red, but richer, fuller, more indefinite. But a closer look threw him into more confusion. It wasn't anything, really. It had no texture, no shadow, and emitted no light despite being so vivid and bright compared to the surrounding darkness. It's as if the object was simply a color, infinite within its confines.

"What is it?"

"It's a fragment of the sunset."

Elijah nearly dropped the jar. He looked back up at the old man and no longer had the courage to doubt him.

"You—You're the Color Merchant!"

"I'd prefer it if you could call me 'Color Doctor' instead."

Elijah's gaze darted between the Color Merchant and his "prescription."

"I can't," he said. He held the jar back out to the merchant even as his stomach twisted and every instinct screamed at him to keep it. "I'm not trading you my soul to cure a blindness that I don't even think I have."

"I told you, I'm a doctor. Not a merchant."

Was it Elijah's imagination, or did he sound annoyed?

The Color Merchant sighed and said something no merchant would say, "This is free. A doctor is meant to heal, after all."

"Who are you trying to fool? We both know nothing's ever free."

"Well, of course, there's a price, but you won't be paying me. Originally, sunsets belonged to us all anyway." The Color Merchant shook his head, put his hands in his coat pockets, and looked up at the city cavern's stone ceiling. What was that look in his eyes? Elijah wondered. He must be comparing the Underground's stone sky to the real one above. What was he seeing beyond the darkness? Elijah wanted to see it, too.

4

The merchant continued, "You can choose whether you want to use the jar or not. You won't know what the price of sight is until you *have* sight."

Elijah looked at the jar. It was so tiny in his hand. So delicate. His eyes fixated on the shard of sunset. He didn't understand how it would cure him. He didn't understand how he could possibly be blind.

And maybe that was the issue. The subtle, nagging force in the back of Elijah's mind took hold of him. He knew it was more than curiosity that pushed him to carefully take the lid of the jar between his fingers and unscrew it. More than his wish to see the sunset, the sky, it was a type of thirst, a type of despair, that only hope could bring.

Elijah opened the jar.

Everything became orange. The boy could no longer see the buildings around him, the Color Merchant, or himself. He couldn't see at all, actually, for his eyes had become a part of the orange, too. The boy was a floating soul. And the orange was so deep, so ripe. This must be what true fire looked like. The kind of fire that belonged in a god's hearth. And the Color Merchant had given it to him instead. The boy was going to drown in it, he was sure. But it was warm. And the warmth hugged the boy like a rind. And the warmth was the boy. And the boy could sleep here. And the boy could dream here. And the boy realized that he didn't mind drowning here. And the boy—

Elijah blinked. The orange shattered and fell into oblivion around him. He was standing on solid ground in the alleyway again, the bag of groceries leaning against his feet.

The Color Merchant was gone.

The world had shifted, somehow. It had fallen. Elijah could feel it: the void in every shallow breath, the missing colors, the missing possibilities. Their absence seared themselves into his memory. The cavern's stone ceiling loomed above him, higher than anything he would ever reach. Elijah could still feel the shard of sunset tickling his skin, seeping through the space between his ribs, filling his lungs.

Elijah looked down at his trembling hands and wondered if it was all real. A wail bubbled up in his throat from somewhere deep, ready to burst. He curled his hands into fists, watching the shadows of every crease in his skin deepen and fold before suddenly looking around in a panic.

The glass jar, where did it go? Elijah had wanted to inspect it. What if some color remained inside, unescaped?

But he couldn't even hope. The jar had disappeared, too.

The Heart Fable

Once upon a time, there was a village where everyone's hearts were made of metal. Some had hearts of iron and walked around with fisted, guarded looks. Others had hearts of mercury and kept shops or ran errands around town, cunning and fleet-footed.

The formation started in adolescence when a child's moldable flesh began to harden, growing walls around their soul. They were taught that the heart was their soul's embodiment, so it became customary for people to go about their days clad in the metals that matched their hearts, from bracelets to piercings to clothes laced with metal thread. They strode through the streets, each a glimmering star. Those with hearts too ugly or common to be forged into something valuable simply displayed nothing and were deemed lesser.

The village kept a record book of all the known metal hearts, from nickel to brass, zinc to tin, and who had which. But while the people had gotten quite good at differentiating them, no one could be truly sure about the substance of another's soul. Thus, there came a tradition that upon a person's death, their heart was extracted to reveal their true self. The adults did it to have peace of mind. The children—who had yet to grow hearts—made it a game, betting pieces of candy against each other at funerals and triumphantly (or dejectedly) walking away. The adolescents looked solemnly upon each reveal of a lesser metal and prayed for a heart they would be proud to call their own. In this way, funerals become public town events.

In this village, there lived a young jeweler who was acknowledged throughout the town as having the one true heart of gold. While many people *claimed* to have a heart of gold after going to a diviner or studying their horoscopes, a true golden heart emerged through one's actions, not through declaration, which made the jeweler's heart all the more veritable.

The jeweler's shop in the corner of the town square was always flooded with people. Her customers figured that whatever she made would be of the highest quality. All the richest and noble families desired her services and attended public events clad from head to toe in her workmanship. Perhaps it was only because she was gold-hearted that the village let her become a jeweler in the first place. Those with hearts hewn from lesser metals were usually barred from such important occupations. Whether there was a difference in quality or not, the jeweler put her all into her work, each ornament infused with a bit of her soul.

No one could remember who started calling the jeweler gold-hearted. It just sort of happened, and over the years, it became a truth. But the signs were always there. As a child, she had been helpful and proactive around town, lending everyone a hand or an ear. As she grew older, her skillset only increased. *Need marital advice? Ask the jeweler. No, she isn't married, but her recommendations are universal! Need someone to watch your kids while you visit the market? The gold jeweler, she'll take them. Need consolation? Miss Gold will rest your mind. Need anything? Miss Gold would do it best.*

Sometimes, gold really felt like the solution to everything, especially in the jeweler's line of work. Ladies would queue outside her shop, each fretting over some kind of invisible ugliness they *knew* they had. And maybe because Miss Gold wasn't a doctor, she never saw any symptom of ugliness beyond their vocalizations of it. She simply cut their jewelry, each curl of a bronze leaf, each link of a silver chain, imbued with all the beauty she could muster.

One winter, the village head's daughter wandered into her shop. The girl, barely ten years of age, stumbled through the doorway, pompously brushing snowflakes from her shoulders as if she had returned home. She carried herself like a stray cat, proud and wary.

She crept up to the counter where Miss Gold sat. "Hello. Everyone says you're good at answering questions."

The jeweler chuckled. "I wouldn't say I'm good at it, but I always try. Ask away."

"I was wondering, does the person define the heart, or does the heart define the person?"

Miss Gold studied the girl. She was a peculiar child, glowing with curiosity—as most children did before their hearts solidified— beneath a rigid mask of dignity that came with her station.

"What's your name?"

"Catherine," the girl said. Then she added, "My papa's the village head."

"Well, Catherine, I'm afraid I don't have an answer. It's a topic I never really considered."

"Really? Not even when you were little, like me?"

"No, I was concerned about... other things." The jeweler smiled. "I'll mull it over and give you an answer another day."

Catherine frowned. Adults, especially the type who associated with her father, usually said that exact phrase when they wanted her to drop the subject. But she didn't feel that way with Miss Gold. Miss *Gold*. She nodded instead.

"Can I find you tomorrow?"

"Visit anytime you wish."

And so the next day Catherine came back and left answer-less. And the day after, and the day after that, each day for the next four years. Soon, Miss Gold's "I'm sorry, I still don't have an answer" became an expectation. So, Catherine stopped asking. Instead, she would spend hours meandering about the periphery of the small shop, where Miss Gold displayed several dozen of her best creations in quaint glass cabinets. Catherine always managed to find new details in each piece, no matter how many times she had looked at it before.

She marveled at Miss Gold's smelting, at the way metal bent to her will. She observed each silver and bronze-hearted individual—many of whom she personally knew—trudge into the shop, burdened by some perceived fault they believed could be masked by jewelry.

But despite the customer's personal insecurities, no one ever commented on the jeweler's appearance. Miss Gold's facial structure didn't align well, and her time spent forging and shaping metal had made her bulky and muscular, especially in the arms and shoulders. She also had a hunched back, disfigured from all the nights she spent bent over the crafts table. When compared to the jewelry she made, Miss Gold could even be called ugly. But it didn't matter, not to Catherine. There was a deeper beauty stored inside her, brighter than the Sun.

Yet, over the years, simply observing wasn't enough for Catherine. Simply *living* wasn't enough. Something was missing. Catherine would trudge home sometimes and pause in the middle of the street, suddenly baffled by the physics that let her control her own limbs. When she sat through her parents' admonishments or compliments, she never felt any of their words land. Her friends' voices came through muffled as if shouted upwind.

"It's just a phase," Miss Gold said, peering at a work-in-progress set of cufflinks.

"Really?"

"Children tend to feel estranged when they reach adolescence and start growing hearts."

Growing a heart. Catherine slumped down on the counter, head on her arms. She peeked at Miss Gold through strands of fallen hair and sulked.

"You still haven't given me an answer."

The jeweler didn't look at her but furrowed her brow in response.

Catherine huffed, "My question! Does the person define the heart, or does the heart define the person? You said you would give me an answer someday, and it's been four years!"

Miss Gold's calloused hands halted. She examined the adolescent girl leaning across the counter. The stray cat from all those years ago was still a stray, but her pride had long since faded to desperation.

"This is about a gold heart, isn't it?"

When Miss Gold's eyes met hers, Catherine lowered her gaze and stammered, "I just want to know. I've tried doing what you're doing. I've tried to help people and be as nice as possible. At my school, around town, I tried so hard! But no one's saying I'm gold! Is it because I'm doing something wrong? Or is it predestined?"

The jeweler looked down at the half-finished necklace she was making, each golden leaf carefully molded and trimmed under smoldering heat, and shook her head.

"I don't know, Catherine. Sometimes, answers are beyond our ability to find. Sometimes, answers need the right person to say them. Sometimes, there are simply no answers at all. All I know is that I have none."

"Then, do you have a way to help me get a gold heart?"

"Why do you want one so badly?"

Catherine couldn't find the words. She took in the kind yet exhausted lines stretching across Miss Gold's face, marring her youth. But those lines were accomplishments, testaments to her standing. Walk into any house in the village, and in the lady's cabinet, there will be jewelry made by Miss Gold.

And what about Catherine? When other villagers recognized her, they saw first her father— "Look, that's the village head's daughter! Hasn't she grown to be a beautiful and bright young woman? And she's so mature. Her parents have raised her well. She'll be a bronze,

I bet, or maybe even a silver." Silver? The village had dozens of them. No, Catherine had to be gold.

"I just want something that belongs to me, something to put my name on."

The door swung open, and a middle-aged lady sauntered in before pausing. "Is this a bad time?"

Miss Gold sprang up. "Of course not, Madam Rena. I have your order right here."

"Splendid! Thank you, Miss Gold." The lady's countenance glowed like polished platinum. Madam Rena shredded the parcel's outer wrapping and lifted up a dazzling pair of earrings with five gleaming leaves, each arranged in a star-shape and inlaid with small emeralds. Catherine, barely an arm's width away, sucked in a breath. She watched Madam Rena try the earrings on and watched her beam. At that moment, the lady seemed even brighter than Miss Gold.

When Madam Rena left the shop, her head held a foot taller than when she entered. Catherine turned to the jeweler. "Miss Gold, I want to commission the most beautiful gold necklace in the world so that I'll shine just like Madam Rena did. But even more."

"That's not how you get a gold heart, Catherine."

"But what else can I do? I've done everything I can to increase my chances."

The jeweler faltered, recognizing the walls of denial calcifying around Catherine's soul.

"Please help me, Miss Gold. Really, just this once," the young woman promised. "Just so I can prove gold fits me. You know how important this is to me."

Miss Gold searched Catherine's eyes. She had never understood her obsession with a gold heart. As long as Miss Gold lived, her heart would never belong to just herself. People would always covet it, clawing through the shop door to get a piece of her. Catherine craved the attention granted by a golden heart without realizing how much she would have to give away. That's the problem.

Maybe Miss Gold would just show her. She nodded. "Alright."

It was like a spell had broken. Catherine's face broke into a wide, relieved smile. She straightened up and bowed her head. "Thank you!"

When Catherine left the shop that evening, all Miss Gold could see was that smile. It hung in the corner of her vision; in the halo of each candle, the shadows cast onto the floor. It was the same smile of her previous customer, and the one before that, and so on.

She got up and paced, coming to a stop before the gallery of necklaces around the shop. Her greatest creations, never worn by a soul, are perpetually displayed to dazzle newcomers with their beauty. To draw attention away from her own appearance.

Miss Gold touched a finger to her cheek. Before she was Miss Gold, she had been a plain child living on the outskirts of the village. Unbecoming and scrawny to the bone, people said, which made jewelling all the more appealing. At least it proved that she still had beauty left inside her, and that she could still be desired, if not for her appearance, then for her talents and skill. So the plain child ran around town helping everyone out, desperate to show the world what she could offer, what she could be.

Maybe that's why she and Catherine had become so close. They both wanted to be noticed. But Miss Gold tried to prove herself by making others beautiful, and Catherine by obtaining a gold heart. What had been an accidental boon to the jeweler set an example for the hopeful girl instead. In the end, maybe it really was all Miss Gold's fault. She stared out the shutters at the rainstorm beyond her shop walls.

Having failed to satisfy Catherine's question, the least Miss Gold could do now was make her a piece of jewelry. She sat back down before her desk and smoothed out a blank piece of paper. For Catherine, this necklace would have to be a masterpiece. It would have to be pure gold, no doubt, maybe inlaid with orange-pink jewels for depth. It should be minimalist, befitting Catherine's age, but also maintain a sense of otherworldliness. Should it be a pendant type or a collar type? How thick? How thin?

In such a manner, Miss Gold sketched away through the night. At dawn, she fuzzily stumbled to the door and put up a handwritten notice: *Closed for three days*. Not even when Catherine came knocking did she leave her work. She ate through her store of emergency provisions, slept fitfully against an ash-covered pillow, and flinched when a little sunlight filtered in through the window shades and reflected off her metals. Miss Gold worked and worked, shaping each curve to perfection, pouring every ounce of warmth into the necklace. Catherine's smile haunted her at every step.

On the third day, Miss Gold lifted the finished necklace with trembling, exhausted fingers. The pendant hung heavy and cool. She tried letting it flash in the light. But it didn't. There was something dull about it, almost gilded. The ghost of Catherine's smile hung in the air, looking unimpressed. It would never be good enough, Miss Gold realized. No jewelry would ever fill an empty heart.

But she had nothing left to offer.

Clutching the necklace, Miss Gold laid her head between her arms and rested for what felt like the first time since she picked up a pair of pliers as a child.

On the fifth day, a queue of townsfolk had lined up at her door, each with their own wants and hopes. It was mid-summer, and the heat only added fuel to their fervent needs. When Miss Gold still showed no sign of movement, the queue became angry. The queue became a mob. They broke her shop door down, but their anger dissipated when a sour smell wafted from the dark shop interior. Lying with its head between its arms, in a napping position, was Miss Gold's two-day-old corpse. The villagers carried the body outside. From the sidelines, a certain adolescent girl watched with a sick horror.

One of the townsfolk noticed Miss Gold's hand and pried open her fingers to retrieve a dazzling pendant necklace. On the back, it was engraved: "To you, my gold-hearted." There was no specified name.

They showed the necklace to everyone, searching for the intended owner with a gold heart. When no one stepped forth to claim it, the villagers decided it should be buried with Miss Gold, a final testament to her legacy.

At the funeral, Catherine couldn't help but approach the coffin. The entire village was there, but she had no problem passing through the crowd as if she had become a ghost. She laid a hand on the open casket, marveled at how her fingers didn't feel like hers, and stared at the gray, foreign face caked in soot. Catherine laid her other hand over her own chest and felt nothing there.

The funeral surgeon came through with the heart retrieval knife and bent over Miss Gold. Catherine could hear the vague chittering of younger children at the edge of the crowd, placing their bets on the nature of the jeweler's heart. She clenched her fist. How *dare* they bet? Did they realize who lay in the casket? Did it even make sense to bet?

It was over quickly. The sharp tip of the knife dug into the corpse. Catherine didn't look away, didn't even blink. The surgeon reached in and plucked out Miss Gold's heart.

Catherine squinted. Was it just the sun in her eyes, or was the heart gray-colored? The town drew a collective breath. Each person flipped through their memories, analyzing how they had gotten it so wrong. The ladies who had worn her jewelry to the funeral traced the metallic leaves on their bracelets, their floral hair clips, and the mini chains woven into their outfits with dread. How could it be? Had Miss Gold deceived the town, or had the town deceived her? Could they even call her Miss Gold now?

All around, there was the silent crack and snap of judgments. For the heart in the surgeon's hand, held aloft for all to see, wasn't gold, but instead, a crumbling hunk of lead.

Through blurring eyes, Catherine traced the heart's shriveled outline. Was this the answer Miss Gold could never give?

Suddenly, Catherine felt something igniting in her chest. It smoldered and melted into an indescribable, poisonous substance, a writhing mess of contradiction and forgery. She winced and hunched down, reaching out blindly for something to hold on to and grasping only the cold, solid rim of Miss Gold's casket. The pain was so bright, burning like a star. All Catherine could do was close her eyes and wish for darkness.

The End.

The Queen of America

For Zaux, the Thasu Intergalactic Space Station was a nightmare that came to life. He wasn't particularly timid, but he was a xur—a blue biped with a distinguishing trait of intense agoraphobia. He stood on the New Arrivals Platform #3460 as it navigated the railway system that orbited the artificial planet like a giant web and watched the scenery pass by.

From a distance, the central Space Station was lively and bursting with color, with hundreds of spaceships departing and arriving. What looked like sluggish bacteria from above were actually hundreds of mingling species, some thrice Zaux's height or the size of his foot, some slithering, some rolling in water-filled globes.

Throughout Zaux's career as a diplomat, he became one of the few individuals of his entire species to have visited over 3,000 stations. Not the best job for someone with agoraphobia, but since it was a species-wide issue, the bonuses for being a sacrificial lamb were always welcome! Even so, the amount of emergency meetings was getting on his nerves, especially with his new promotion. By all standards, once he became an *ambassador,* he should have gotten his own private ship straight to the United Intergalactic Alliance headquarters. But given the last-minute notice and the fact that he had been vacationing in a relatively remote galaxy, Zaux was shoved back into the agony of space station crowds.

As Zaux's platform slowed and veered onto a branching rail, his headset filled his ears with frantic notifications from his superiors. His current mission really gave him a headache. Something about a recently emerged species wiping out half their galaxy and about to colonize the rest. The emergency meeting was still a few dozen galaxies away.

The platform landed with a jolt. Zaux followed the crowds as they began streaming into the main commercial hub of the space station.

17

He sucked in a deep breath and stepped outside. The noise and lights hit him like the after-flares of a rocket engine, and he felt his stomach lurch.

"Move it." A not-so-gentle nudge from behind prompted Zaux to keep going. He shook off his paralyzed muscles and eased off the platform landing pad, shuddering with each step and flailing his four arms about to make way. It was a strategy that worked often.

From there, he made his way to the station's highest-rated food alley. Zaux had just enough time to catch a bite before boarding his transfer flight and being subjected to more horrid spaceship meals. He wanted both a good restaurant and an empty one, which was difficult since the best ones were always packed. He was about to give up before he saw it: an empty restaurant hidden in the shadow of its behemoth neighbor. Zaux almost doubted it was in service, but the wide open door told him otherwise.

Zaux squinted at the name in large, red, bold letters, written in the Universal language. "The Queen of…" He frowned and sounded out, "Ah-mur-ee-cah."

From the ceiling hung a series of bell-shaped lamps. Red stripes lined the walls, interrupted by two giant menu boards. A figure wearing a matching red uniform waved at Zaux from behind the counter.

The worker had pale skin, two arms, two legs, and very long fingers. On their head was a bundle of—purple hair. For most species, the color was too flashy for survival. Two arched stripes of hair above their two eyes? Unusual but not unseen. A… triangular shaped breathing hole—no, *two* breathing holes jutting out the front of their face? Fascinating.

The worker opened their mouth, and Zaux's headset translated, "Welcome to the Queen of America! Could I get you anything to eat?"

As soon as they were done speaking, they stretched their lips back to reveal a row of straight, yellowish teeth and bared them aggressively at Zaux. He shuddered, then reminded himself that different species had different customs. From the way their message was translated, Zaux was pretty sure it was a gesture of friendliness.

Almost as soon as that thought passed, a sonorous beep signifying the second-to-highest level danger alert from his headpiece, which had finished sorting through a database worth trillions of species, filled all six of his ears. Zaux stiffened, fixating on the worker as his headpiece fed him the relevant species profile.

A homo sapiens sapiens? With a total existence of less than a thousandth of xurs' *recorded* existence, homo sapiens sapiens— gonochoristic, warm-blooded, highly aggressive, and unpredictable bipeds that exhibit limited-to-extreme speciesism among varying individuals—have waged almost septuple the number of wars. And just like how "xur" was a more convenient version of "Xeraphnitushsrwu," these creatures were also more commonly known as "humans."

Zaux *knew* he had heard the term "homo sapiens sapiens" somewhere! In his current mission briefing about a newly integrated, genocidal species, no less. Great.

The worker noticed Zaux's hesitation and tilted their head. "Are you alright?"

He realized he had been staring and shook his head. No matter what sort of species he was facing, it would be rude not to adhere to the universal etiquette—which boiled down to simply answering each other's questions, using formalities, and staying calm while withholding judgment. And more, if this human was one of the more belligerent of their species, he didn't want to cause unnecessary trouble.

"Of course. I was wondering about the name of your restaurant. Is it a place from your home?"

"Yep! America is the origin of fast food culture!"

So that's how it's pronounced. "Does your menu cater to the tastes of specific species?"

"We try to keep it as authentic as possible, although it's inevitable that our ingredients are toxic to some individuals."

"What about xurs?"

"Um, let me check." The worker searched on their hologram interface. They tapped their chin. "As far as I can tell, xurs and humans have similar palettes. Probably."

Well, *that* was reassuring. Zaux eyed the different translated phrases on the men—hamburger, hot dog, grilled cheese, chicken nuggets, milkshake—but recognized none of them. "What would you recommend?"

"Are you looking for a meal or something to drink?"

"Both. Whatever you think is best."

"Okay, one pizza and sparkling lemonade coming right up! You can't go wrong with any of them!" The worker muttered and made a sound... a laugh? And scurried away to the kitchen.

Zaux found himself a seat and mulled over what the worker said while he waited. A *sparkling*—something. Gemstones sparkle. He sure hoped his drink wouldn't have gems in it. And what was that about a home country? He hadn't heard the word "country" in a long time. As an intergalactic diplomat, he usually dealt with planets, star zones, and galaxies.

And the worker, too, was not what he expected. They were nice, very polite and enthusiastic. Zaux had a hard time believing that their species was supposedly committing genocide across their galaxy. Maybe this worker was an anomaly? But then, any species can be driven the wrong way by malicious leadership.

The worker stumbled out from the kitchen, holding a steaming plate and a cup filled with light yellow, bubbly liquid.

"Here's your pizza and sparkling lemonade!" The worker whisked the plate and cup in front of Zaux. The "pizza" was a circular flatbread about as wide as the worker's head, covered with some strange, creamy white and red goo. A combination of smells assaulted Zaux's olfactory senses. He took a sip of the yellow drink first, then, not finding himself a fan of its texture, turned to the pizza. He sniffed and prodded at the goo with his finger.

"That's cheese—mozzarella, specifically," the worker explained.

Zaux didn't bother trying to figure out what the chatty worker was saying anymore and raised the entire pizza, about to take a bite.

"Wait! Don't—"

Zaux swallowed it whole.

"Oh." The worker's eyes went wide.

The taste was interesting, to say the least. But the texture was heavenly. Whatever this mozzarella was, it had the potential to be an intergalactically popular food. He looked down at the now empty plate.

"It was delicious. But rather small."

"You ate that entire pizza in one bite?"

"Hardly a bite."

The worker swallowed, then seemed to brighten. "Well, I can make you another one, esteemed customer."

"How about 15 more? And just call me Zaux."

21

"Alright, Zaux!" The worker saluted, laughed gleefully, and raced away to the kitchen again. "Ella Jones at your service—15 pizzas coming right up!"

Ella came out with 16 instead. "One for me," she clarified. "I can't just watch you eat it all without eating any myself! My grandma always said: If you're sad, eat it to make you happy. If you're happy, eat it to make you happier. If you're with a friend, eat it together. I haven't been able to have a pizza eating session in a while 'cause no one here really appreciates human food."

Zaux nodded, munching on his sixth pizza. "How exactly do you have such an unpopular restaurant here? Isn't the rent on space stations insane?"

"My family's rich. They supported my dream of becoming a restaurant owner. I thought human food would take off," Ella mumbled as she took a minuscule bite of her own pizza. "All the non-humans I met back home said it would explode in popularity, so I wanted to catch the tide. Looks like I was too early, though. My family runs another branch in my home galaxy, Galaxy BX198, which is just starting to turn a profit."

Wait, hadn't Zaux just read a mission briefing about BX198? This was a good opportunity to get a native's opinion. He probed, "You mean the galaxy where that war is about to break out?"

"Where a what?"

Zaux expertly hid his surprise. "A war. Well, the brink of war. It's all over the news."

"Huh. I haven't heard anything about it. Who's the aggressor? Humans?"

"Yeah. So I've heard."

Ella nodded her focus elsewhere. Zaux could almost see a loading bar in her brain. Then she took a bite of her pizza, chewed a bit, and said something he never expected:

"Guess they're at it again."

"Sorry?"

Ella kept munching. "Humans have been squabbling a bunch with our other galactic neighbors over the years. Doesn't help that our government's basically a bunch of old people a couple of lifetimes overdue for retirement. Hey, don't you sometimes think to yourself, technology is awesome? Like, my grandma's four times as old as the average lifespan for humans from *before* our species' intergalactic integration..."

Zaux almost wondered if the human he met was a little too scatterbrained. Instead of focusing on a *galactic* war concerning her species, she'd gone on a tangent about anti-aging technology.

"...But I get to live even longer than that since I've been taking those pills since I was an adolescent—"

"Wait, wait." Zaux held up a hand.

"Something wrong? Sorry, I must be talking too much, right?"

"I was just a bit surprised by your reaction. Most individuals would freak out if they found out their species was on the brink of a galactic war. But you're so, well, nonchalant."

"It's not like it's a surprise. Our history is full of wars. Besides, what am *I* supposed to do about it? I'm just a restaurant owner on a space station almost a hundred galaxies away from BX198."

"But your family—"

"My grandma's on a business trip even farther away from BX198. My parents are sightseeing somewhere, and I forgot about the planet."

"And your friends?"

"They're mostly studying across the universe."

"So your attachment to humanity—"

"Attachment? I guess I'm a little concerned, but not that much." Ella shrugged and took a bite of her pizza. "I told you, humans are violent. In the time I've opened shop here, we had already waged several star-system-level wars. Galactic's just a bigger scale, right?"

"A *lot* bigger," he emphasized. For some reason, the way Ella so casually dismissed *any* sort of war made Zaux's diplomatic pride itch. His remaining three pizzas sat forgotten.

"Right, a lot bigger. But that's just the way war is. You win some, you kill some. It's tragic but common."

"But it can be prevented," Zaux protested.

"Sure, it can, but you gotta be in charge to do that. As far as I can tell, I'm definitely *not* in charge of humanity, and even if I were, I'd quit right away. Politics are just a bunch of old geezers with inflated egos playing cards with people's lives as betting chips."

Zaux got the gist of her reference. "Politics is more than that! As we speak, leaders throughout the universe are working tirelessly to achieve peace. Without the United Intergalactic Alliance, without civic negotiations, budding civilizations like yours would have been crushed by intergalactic proxy wars long ago. Petty squabbles would escalate into destroyed star systems. Trillions of lives would be lost!"

Ella's brows jumped half her forehead. "How, exactly, do you know these guys have everyone's best interests in mind? How do you know there aren't disgusting power plays and corruption going on behind the scenes?"

"Because they're honorable, responsible people."

"Whoa. How much are you getting paid to say this?"

"I'm not being—" Zaux took a deep breath. "How about we turn the question around? Why are you so doubtful of the powerful?"

"Well, it's only natural: where there's power, there's corruption. Removal from the masses. People lose empathy."

Zaux stared, thought some, then stared some more. Ella really looked like she believed what she was saying. It was strange. "What sort of political environment are you used to?"

"Well, my country was a democracy, and we had two main parties, but the officials on both sides were always attacking the other party and never got anything done. There was always a bunch of drama, and overall, it was just ugly. I learned to stay out of that stuff."

Zaux remembered America now. It was a former country briefly mentioned in the mission overview document he had skimmed while on the spaceship. According to the United Intergalactic Alliance's predictions, humanity's origin planet had been on course for an extinction-level event due to nuclear warfare. Hence why, the local Alliance branch made contact back then largely to prevent it. The irony that the species they saved was starting a galactic war at this very moment wasn't lost on him.

"I suppose your pessimism is warranted." Zaux picked up his remaining pizzas, now lukewarm, and continued munching.

"What about you? Why are you so optimistic about the government?"

Zaux looked at Ella. Ella was an ordinary person. An ordinary human. And Zaux? A political figure headed to a conference where her species would be the central topic. His earlier hunch was correct; meeting her here *was* an opportunity. He made a choice. "Well, because I'm a part of it. I work as an ambassador at the United Intergalactic Alliance."

25

"Oh," Ella paused. "Makes sense then. Sorry if I offended you."

"No, no, it's alright."

"So, do you interact a lot with other government officials? Is there a lot of corruption? I mean, *you* don't look corrupt, but you know."

"All I can say is, most people are decent. On such a universal level, you don't get to the top by fighting with your colleagues. There's a lot of responsibility that comes with being involved in decision-making on an intergalactic level. Screw up once, and you're out. Doesn't matter the backer; there's always someone more powerful. The universe is boundless."

"Hm, I guess national and intergalactic are two different levels."

Zaux continued, "So on this topic, let's say an ambassador working for the United Intergalactic Alliance wanted to know more about humans—you know, the type of stuff that they *don't* tell you in classified files and would be important in a diplomatic meeting about humanity's recent actions. What would you tell them?"

Zaux hoped he wasn't putting pressure on her. Turned out he had nothing to worry about. Ella made a sharp guttural sound—which Zaux's headset translated into visual text: *clearing the pharynx of mucosa*—and took a deep breath.

She started, "Well, humans have quite a rich culture, I suppose. Let's start with one of my favorite stories…"

And Zaux, the newly promoted xur ambassador, missed his spaceship for the first time in his career.

***

The twelve-eyed attendant behind the desk looked at Zaux, a look that made him squirm underneath his thick, diplomacy-hardened skin. Then, she shifted her gaze to look at the automated dolly behind him that carried a stack of pizza boxes taller than himself, each box wider than his arm span.

The pizzas had taken quite a while to make and weren't exactly cheap. Once Ella had found out Zaux was ordinarily wealthy, she doubled the prices and still had the nerve to call it a discount, claiming her original intention was to triple them. But Zaux was a friend now, and friends did each other favors. Needless to say, Zaux had learned something *else* intrinsic to humans.

The attendant seemed to study the pizza stack phenomena for a moment, then swiveled back to the paperwork as if the strangeness was beyond her paycheck.

She sent him his new tickets through the AI interface and promptly kicked him out. Zaux found himself in suffocating crowds once more, but this time, others cleared the way for the giant stack of pizza rolling in front of him. In his mind, he replayed the stories Ella had told him: a princess who had interspecies friendships with animals that most humans considered vermin, an aquatic version of humans, and a vigilante who could shoot sticky webs from his fingertips.

Lost in the stories, Zaux barely processed the swirl of lights and movement around him. Finding a partial cure for his innate agoraphobia wasn't something Zaux had expected when he stepped off his spaceship earlier. But ordinary people could surprise you sometimes, and space stations were full of them.

The Ending

For a giant world map poster:

I feel the tape on my borders ripped away. My owner folds me in half and then once more. And again and again until I— I who once covered an entire wall— am reduced to a little less than two square feet. He stacks me with my brethren inside a cardboard box. I am the last poster, the top of the pile.

I was also the first poster. For three decades, I watched over this classroom. Day after day, year after year. Every morning before my owner arrives and every night after the last student leaves, I stay. I live here.

I *lived* here. I glimpse the bare walls for a final time, the only things that've been in this classroom longer than me. The cold flaps of the box fold in, and then the world goes dark.

For a particular student:

I ease the door open, and an alien sight greets me: blank, off-white colored walls, large boxes scattered throughout, and a— Whoa, that's a huge ball of crumpled duct tape sitting on his desk. If not for Mr. Johnson pacing around, I'd think I entered the wrong room.

He sees me and stops, asking, "Isn't school over? What are you still doing here?"

I fidget and suddenly remember the farewell card I'm holding. "This," I say. I hold it out for Mr. Johnson.

He takes it and doesn't seem to realize what it is. "Oh, and…?"

"Congratulations on your retirement."

Mr. Johnson looks at me, eyes bulging and mouth slightly agape, an expression I've never seen him wear before. Usually, he's like a fresh corpse that someone has dragged out from the grave and slapped a wig on, expressionless and dull. Maybe retirement, or rather, the prospect of retirement, gave him some fresh energy.

Several heartbeats passed. Pretty awkward. Why did I think this was a good idea again?

Then, Mr. Johnson tilts his head and asks slowly, pronouncing each syllable, "For me? Really?"

I nod. I hope he likes the card. I even drew a quick, messy sketch of the Palace of Versailles on the inside. King Louis XIV of France is his second favorite historical figure. I forgot his favorite— more like I was doodling and didn't pay attention when he mentioned it— and didn't feel like asking anyone.

Mr. Johnson examines the envelope. For a few seconds, he looks confused. Then, he mumbles something I cannot hear.

"Uh, could you repeat it, please?" I lean in closer.

He says, "I'm sorry."

Sorry? Now, I'm the one who's confused. "For what?"

Mr. Johnson scratches his chin as if deciding whether or not to answer. Then, he responds, "For leaving."

I almost forget to reply. Is he sorry for leaving?

"It's okay," I stammer. I realize I've been unconsciously fidgeting with my hands and back out of the room, giving Mr. Johnson a final wave. Hopefully, he will have a stress-free retirement. I can name quite a few classmates who have been absolute headaches this past year.

Speaking of which, I gotta hurry to my new summer job. It's actually got a decent salary. Today's my first day, and I'm sure I'll be off to a good, fresh start.

For a trash can:

That teacher read the card for a long time before he lifted his head and gazed at the doorway for even longer. Then, he walked towards a certain picture frame on his desk, picked it up with both hands and removed the picture inside.

I felt the conviction in his footsteps as he strode over to me. Objects come to me to die.

He looked down at the photo in his hands, expressionless, and then let go. It was strange. The photo was probably older than this school itself, but even after such a long passage of time, the colors hadn't faded. In the picture, the teacher was wearing a tuxedo and stood next to a young woman in a white dress. I didn't recognize her. Maybe it was just the blurred lines of a low-res print, but the teacher looked different in the photo: younger, dashing, and vibrant.

For an analog clock:

He doesn't leave immediately. Instead, he sits in his cushioned chair and looks towards the doorway as if waiting for someone— another student, perhaps? Or someone else? Who knows what that man is thinking.

An hour passes. Then two. Specifically, two hours, seven minutes, and forty-seven seconds. The sun sets, and the security guards of the school begin to lock the doors. The man continues to wait. No one comes. I don't know what he's still doing here. He seems to be a little crazy. Or desperate. Time does a number on the human mind. And he's got quite a bit of time under his belt.

Finally, the man stands up, looking a little stiff. I can almost hear his joints creaking like unoiled door hinges. The man sweeps his gaze across the room one last time and turns away. Maybe he finally realizes how suffocating bare walls can be. Then, he stacks three cardboard boxes together, picks them up, and staggers out of the classroom on uneven legs. His neck lurches from side to side as if he's wandering through a dream. The last I ever see of that man is his boot heel, vanishing into the darkness of the halls.

This is the ending for an ordinary man. Or maybe the start. The void he leaves behind fills the room. Everything falls still— except for my hands. Ticking and ticking. There's no ending for me.

Mission Melody

I'm sitting in the very back row of the van, trying to perfect my hand shadow puppets.

Alyssa, my fellow backseat sufferer, examines my progress and nods. She's been teaching me these shadow puppets for the past two hours. Bookless, too weary to talk, and with everyone's electronics confiscated by the camp supervisors, there's little else two awkward teens squished in a van headed to the middle of nowhere can do.

Alyssa demonstrates the next shadow puppet, hanging her fingers in a limp C shape with one hand and clasping the other over the back of it and raising her thumb: A wolf, jaw tense, teeth bared, ears perked and haughty. I attempt a replication and come up with something that looks—at best—like a horse. I adjust. Now, it's a crocodile.

I'm vaguely aware of the opening melody of *Yellow* by Coldplay, beginning to play for the fourteenth time. It's a favorite of our camp supervisor and our van-designated theme song.

In the middle row, the three boys in our group are having a heated debate about the usefulness of a video game character. One of them changes the subject to lost socks. I write what they're saying down in my notebook. It's interesting, and my English teacher has always told me to keep a tracker for everything interesting I experience. After a month-long writer's block, I'm ready to get some of my creativity back during this school-sponsored trip.

As we drive higher into the mountains, pine trees begin to fill the Colorado grass fields. Then, patches of snow. In late May. The horizon stretches endlessly. I wonder if we'll drive off the edge of the world.

***

It's sundown when our group arrives at *Mission: Wolf*. We park next to a conspicuously unpainted building, and the second van pulls up behind us with the rest of our group. I wonder what music they played. We line up with our duffels: 14 nerve-frayed, back-sore highschoolers and three adult supervisors who certainly don't get paid enough to deal with us.

The snow has formed a thin, cottony layer over the valley. From where we're parked, I can see the red roofs of a small settlement halfway up the mountain, obscured by smaller hills. A wolf howls. A single, piercing note. Several more join the symphony. I shiver.

A *Mission: Wolf* staffer bundled in a purple coat drives down the hill in a golf cart. When she reaches the bottom, she exchanges words with our head supervisor. I don't catch her name. She glances at the snow, then the sun already disappearing over the distant mountain peaks, and gestures to the unpainted building. That's where we'll be sleeping.

I look at my watch. It's only eight. In California time, it's actually seven—way too early for bed, no matter how I justify it. It feels even stranger to go to bed without worrying about—or even knowing—what's happening tomorrow. No exams. No deadlines. Just me. What am I without these responsibilities?

I look around to find everyone else in a similar trance, numbly unpacking their duffels. Already, some are crawling into sleeping bags to hide from the cold, curled in a fetal position. They've got the right idea. I let my duffel slip off my shoulders and take a deep breath.

Somehow, it feels colder without the extra weight.

***

I realize how sore my body is when I finally sit down. At seven in the morning, our group of students just scaled a muddy hill, probably angled at forty degrees, to reach the main campground. The log bench is still moist from the dew, and the chill seeps into my bones. We're

33

supposed to wait for someone here, but I really don't care—until I see him.

The first thing I notice about the founder of *Mission: Wolf* are his leather boots, which look older than the dirt that clings to their soles. Each step carries a weight to it. His hair is a blend of silver and brown, bleached by the sun.

In my notebook, I write, "Kent Weber would make a good movie elf."

This was before he took us to the wolves.

Our group files into the wolf enclosure and sits on a line of log benches. Yes, it had been a part of the trip description that the school handed out to us at the beginning of the year, but it's the kind of activity that doesn't feel real until it happens.

There are multiple wolf enclosures. And the one we're in the "visitor enclosure," is home to a one-year-old wolf, Ydun, whom the *Mission: Wolf* staffers wanted to make their new mascot.

Forget cats. Ydun is the incarnation of chaos. She barrels in like an ox, somehow running into a log despite the agility of her species, and immediately jumps on Kent. He calms her down with a series of head pats and leads her in our direction.

"Don't pull away when she comes close," he instructs. "She'll follow you and knock you over. Lean forward to meeting her, and you'll be fine."

Ydun pads past us once, twice, circling around the row of benches over and over. She sniffs at Alyssa, who's brimming with every possible ounce of anticipation befitting an avid wolf lover, then turns away. Instead, Ydun veers in my direction. I stiffen as she brushes my knee with her snout. Then, she pounces on me, rearing up on her hind legs and reaching her front out towards my shoulders.

"Holy—" I lean back, trying to push her off.

"Don't do that!" Kent yells in the background. "Push forward! Push forward!"

Push? How? All I can see is Ydun in my face, covering me with her slobber. In my panic, I lurch forward and headbutt her. Hard. She shrinks back with a whine and runs off to Kent.

He chuckles, "Well, that's better than I expected. You gotta do it like this." As Ydun approaches, he crouches, reaches out, and brings her face to his. He stretches his lips back and squares his teeth. The wolf and the man touch their teeth.

I blink, midway through clearing my face of wolf slobber.

"It's how wolves greet each other," Kent explains.

As if on cue, Ydun scurries up to one of the long-term volunteers, who bends down and affectionately bumps their teeth against the wolf's. The process repeats itself with other members of our school trip. One of the freshmen loses control and falls backwards off the log. Ydun is on him in a heartbeat, licking all over his face.

"Did he faint?" One of the volunteers runs up. Ydun's enthusiasm fades to concerned licks, whines, and prods. She probably thought the freshman died. The boy flails his arms and manages to throw her off.

"I tried to play dead," he admits. "I thought she would lose interest."

Kent shakes his head. "That's the one thing you wouldn't want to do. You gotta meet them in the middle. Wild animals will instinctively follow you to the afterlife if they think you aren't being responsive."

***

"Hey." Alyssa sits down next to me.

"Hey," I respond. I'd left the enclosure earlier than everyone else. Never being much of a pet person, Ydun's hyperactivity wore me out.

Alyssa crosses her legs, swinging them back and forth. "Look what I got."

There's a big clump of white wool in her hand. It looks almost suspended in the air, half an inch above her skin.

"Where'd you get that?"

"Ydun! When I reached out to pet her, this just came off. Kent said it's shedding season, so all the soft underfur is loosening."

I take the wool in my hands, kneading it between my fingers into a ball. It poofs right back up. Some strands of wolf fur land on my black sweatpants and cling there.

"I see you've got a decent chunk," says Alex, a senior volunteer at *Mission: Wolf.* He's standing behind us in the woodshop, organizing a toolbox. "Has Kent shown you how to make it into a bracelet yet?"

We look at each other. Alyssa shakes her head. "Sounds cool. Can you teach us?"

He gives us a wry grin and walks over. "Of course. I may not be as good as Kent, but I've got quite a bit of practice under my belt. I made all the bracelets on display in the gift shop."

Alex squats down next to us and takes Alyssa's fur ball. Splitting it into three equal sections, he gives one to each of us and uses his own to demonstrate.

"Kent has this one saying that he really likes: Life is…" He pauses as if waiting for us to answer. Neither of us has a clue, so he chuckles and continues, "The answer is 'physics.' Life is just physics."

He stretches and elongates the ball, then begins to twist it, starting from the middle. It compacts into a string, growing longer and longer. "Everything has an equal and opposite reaction, similar to wolves. You pull back, they push in; you pull in, they push back," Alex explains as he works. When the string is about the length of his forearm, he holds it out to us. "Now, I've got it tight enough. There's a lot of torsion packed in here. So what I'm going to do next..." He lets go of one end, and the string instantly snaps on itself from the center, twining into a natural braid.

"See?" Alex grins, looking pretty smug. "Just physics."

From there, he ties the tips of the braid together to form a bracelet and slips it onto his wrist.

"Now you guys try."

***

"Wolves have better communication skills than most humans." It's another quote from Kent.

As I write, a traumatized wolf paces the special enclosure behind me. Obsidian, a black, shaggy, pure-bred wolf, arrived at *Mission: Wolf* two weeks before us. Raised as a regular dog and transferred to the sanctuary by a well-meaning family, he still hasn't recovered from his abandonment.

A ray of sunlight passes over me, and I look up to see, once more, a sprawling, snow-covered valley. It's our lunch break, and I chose this spot on top of the warehouse's exterior storage boxes precisely because of the view. After a busy morning, we finally have a chance to slow down and appreciate the scenery. It feels unreal. Like a painting. Like *I'm* a painting, just a cluster of coarse brush strokes that suddenly became aware of their place on the canvas.

A snarl causes me to freeze. I twist my head around. Obsidian has his snout pressed against the corner of his enclosure, half a foot away from me. I move closer, hoping to touch him, and he sprints away. I spend the next half hour watching him run counterclockwise along the fence. His enclosure is small compared to the others—around the size of a classroom—and filled with man-made wood obstacles.

He knows exactly when I'm looking at him, even with his back turned, and speeds up his pacing. Do wolves have some kind of sixth sense?

I lean back, resting my aching lower back against the warehouse wall. The clump of wool Alyssa gave me earlier sits unused and squashed beneath my water bottle. I had tried making it into a bracelet earlier, but no matter how I tried to twist the wool, it just wouldn't tighten. I'd ended up with a long, fat "string" that flopped uselessly when I let go.

I set my notebook and pencil down and pick the wool up, studying it. It's surprisingly compact, like cotton. Each individual strand of fur is part of a greater whole. I try again, beginning to twist the fur from a fixed center point. My concentration blocks out the ache in my fingers. All I know is the rhythm of twisting and pulling. I get a hang of the balance—how much to stretch it, how much to let it shrink.

Obsidian stops pacing. His breathing slows. I don't need to turn around to know how close he is. I do, however, see a blur of black fur out of the corner of my eye that tells me he has laid down beside me.

We breathe in harmony. I keep twisting the wolf fur string. It's already as long as my pinkie. Obsidian shifts his head from one paw to another, a strangely human gesture.

I latch onto that thought, but I don't write it in my notebook. It isn't a sentiment I'll forget easily. But what does this mean? Maybe humans have a sixth sense, too.

***

The wolves are hungry. Their howls wake us bright and early at four-thirty in the morning, gradually harmonizing into a lonesome melody.

I remain curled in my sleeping bag, drifting in the liminality between dream and reality. When I finally get up a couple hours later, groggy and puffy-eyed, the sun has just come out from behind the mountain. Traces of the previous night's snow fall off the tent poles as I make my way across the construction area to the unfinished building where Javier, our hiking-specialist supervisor, is making breakfast.

By the time everyone has a full belly, it's eight in the morning. We shoulder our packs, ready for another day of manual field labor and wolf caretaking.

A pick-up truck drives past us as we're walking up the hill. A dense, bloody scent wafts from the tarp-covered back. At the top, the main camp is a flurry of activity: It's Feeding Day.

To mimic wolves' eating habits in the wild, *Mission: Wolf* feeds their residents twice every week: Wednesday and Sunday, over ten pounds of meat for each wolf. The newly dead horses or cows are a donation from local ranchers to the wolf sanctuary, which is ironic because back in the 1900s, ranchers lobbied to exterminate local wolves.

Far up the mountain, a wolf begins to howl. I wonder if it's the same one from this morning. More join in. It's a false hunt for domesticated wolves but rewarding all the same.

Kent is standing in the chaos of butchering prep. The staffers have much to do: pull on those mud boots, make sure you aren't in clean clothes, get out the butchering mats and tools—the waste pile will go over there—unload the truck, sort the meat, hurry up and start butchering 'cause the wolves are starving.

A portion of our group inches closer to watch the process with dizzy excitement. We've never seen so much red in our lives. A scene that wouldn't have shocked our ancestors has become, viewed through modern eyes, a circus.

I stay in the distance, watching the staffers hustle. The sky is a deep, clear blue. A puff of clouds line the horizon, tipping over the distant mountain peaks. There's a good breeze today, too, blowing downwind towards the enclosures—probably the reason why the wolves are so frantic—and over the plains. It feels like God took a piece of heaven and dropped it here, in the middle of Colorado, for the workers cutting up a dead horse.

A pool of blood begins to form, spilling off the mats and trickling along a deep crevice in the ground. I had wrongly assumed that the scarred hilltop was eroded by rain. More streams of blood merge into the main artery until it becomes a languid river, flowing downhill where a patch of grass lies, tall and vivid, swaying at peace with the wind.

***

The supervisors shout orders at us. It's natural to leave carrying a bigger mess in your duffel than when you first arrived. Packing, packing, losing items, and finding them again. Finding bug bites along with them. Finding a fresh, overnight pile of cow dung at the entrance of your tent by accidentally stepping on it. Finding many things, even the ones never registered as lost. No time to organize. You can sort through the mess once you're home.

No breakfast, they say, if we want enough time to see the wolves again. By extension, there is no dish duty. Is this a win or a loss?

We file into the wolf enclosures one last time for a goodbye visit. The weather is a stark contrast from the first day we were here, sweltering and dry. Ydun runs up to us with the morning light bouncing off her fur. I reach out when she passes by and grasp a handful of her wool to make into bracelets on the long car ride back. At least I won't have to resort to shadow puppets anymore.

When Ydun bounds away, her tail wags furiously. What I would give to be able to run free and mindless. What I would give to be a wolf. I wonder if Ydun knows we're leaving. I wonder if any of the other wolves we've met do, too. Will I ever step foot into this abandoned corner of heaven again?

Mission: Wolf feels like the kind of place that will disappear when you leave it. There's only one chance. Kind of like Calypso's island. There's an unassuming majesty to this place, these hills and forests. The harmony achieved between nature and civilization, man and beast, the tamed and the untamed, is a kind of peace like no other.

At the camp's central lodge, our group takes turns using the restroom. Those who are finished gather in the distant hillside parking lot, helping our supervisors strap luggage on top of the vans, but I linger by the central lodge, waiting for Alyssa to finish up.

Below me, on the lodge patio, some of the seasonal volunteers are playing a song. Alex is on the guitar. Another shaggy-bearded volunteer, whom I don't know the name of, is drumming. A girl not much older than me is humming.

I let the music carry me, weightless, into some higher dimension. It's a familiar yet elusive melody as if I've heard it over and over in my past lives, and it had left footprints in my mind.

Monism

One day, everyone's reflections went on strike, and Chloe found out through her college roommate.

Janet popped her head out of the bathroom door and knocked twice on the wall, forcing Chloe to look away from her half-finished marketing project. She was about to remark on Janet's wet hair dripping onto the wooden floorboards but held back when she saw her expression.

"Something up?"

Janet nodded. "The mirror broke."

"You broke it?"

"No. It just broke."

Chloe processed that for a second. "You're telling me the mirror broke itself."

"Yeah," Janet said, her face a shade between confusion and amusement.

Chloe stood up from her swivel chair. "Okay, lemme see."

She stepped past Janet into their bathroom and froze. For a few moments, she couldn't describe what was wrong with the mirror. Her mind couldn't comprehend it. There was nothing in the mirror. Well, the *room* was still there, the counters and makeup palettes, towels and all that, but neither she nor Janet appeared. Chloe side-eyed her roommate.

"Damn, that screen is hyper realistic. How much did it cost?"

"I'm not pranking you!"

"Please get rid of it before I shower, it's—"

"I said, this isn't a trick! I really have no idea how this happened."

"You're telling me that—" Chloe gestured at the mirror, a little angry now, "Our reflections have magically disappeared. And you had nothing to do with it?"

There was a pounding at their door. The two roommates exchanged a glance. Janet opened the door, and there was their next-door neighbor, Sierra.

"Did your reflections disappear?" asked Sierra, panting.

With an I-told-you-so glance at Chloe, Janet responded, "You guys too?"

Sierra cursed in affirmation, and the two pulled up the news, their phone cameras, and social media. In the dorm halls, more students emerged, looking more awake at midnight than any dose of caffeine could've prompted.

Chloe zoned out all their voices, rising in hysteria, and touched a finger to the mirror. It felt just like it always had, except her reflection wasn't there anymore. The mirror looked like a perfect, unpixellated photo of an empty bathroom.

***

The world descended into mayhem. It wasn't just the reflections. Shadows too. Even photos or videos taken in the past turned up empty. It was almost as if humans simply didn't appear on the light spectrum anymore—which also didn't make sense since each human being was just a conglomerate of atoms, no different from the tables or walls that the mirrors still reflected. There was a bug in reality.

Models and actors suddenly found themselves jobless. Animation studios shot to the top of the entertainment industry. News channels showed empty, almost ghostly newsrooms. Videos of presidential speeches featured a disembodied voice speaking from an empty podium to an empty auditorium. YouTube and Instagram became a graveyard of dreary landscapes—abandoned cities in their gray, cement splendor.

In the absence of entertainment, people began going out to parks, digging out old bikes or tennis racquets from storage. Bookstores saw a sharp increase in revenue. Nature documentaries surged in popularity.

Still, others turned to less savory means of busying themselves in their downtime. Criminal activity and drug usage peaked since surveillance systems were handicapped. Each security camera was reduced to monitoring the opening and closing of doors. Photo IDs showed a blank, white background. Airports and border crossings were shut down with iron clamps. Ships were left stranded offshore. Military personnel scrambled to lock down their secret bases.

On the internet, conspiracy theories by newfound cults diffused and crescendo like a digital virus. Overseas, the Pope declared, in a written document, that the disappearance of human reflections was not an indication of the Second Coming and demanded that the populace calm down. No one listened. Dozens of church branches formed overnight, each helmed by a self-proclaimed prophet preaching that they were visited by an angel on the night of the "Great Disappearance."

***

Exactly a month after the reflections disappeared, they came back.

Chloe caught the precise moment hers did. She was in the bathroom, brushing her teeth and staring idly into the mirror. There was no reason to do so, but habits are some of the most durable things to exist. Over the past couple weeks, she had been reading up on spiritualism and different philosophers, especially Nietzsche. He offered a glimmer of rationality and stability through the chaos, which was ironic since he went clinically insane in the latter half of his life.

Then, the mirror warped. The head of the toothbrush, which had been floating in midair, suddenly disappeared, concealed by a pair of lips. The image elongated into a nose, a neckline, eyebrows, and arms like some invisible hand had reverse-erased the image back into existence. Chloe made eye contact with the figure in the mirror.

Her reflection blinked. Chloe's breath lulled. Had she blinked? No, she hadn't. Just to be sure, she held her eyes wide open. They had barely started watering when the reflection blinked again. It raised its hand and pressed on the glass. Like a greeting.

Chloe swore, stumbled out of the bathroom, and slammed the door.

***

Once again, the world upended itself.

Everyone agreed that what came back were not reflections. They were something else.

Many who had been standing in front of their mirrors when these "reflections" returned had vanished off the face of the earth. "Swallowed" is how witnesses described it on social media sites and the news. There was no video evidence; people were swallowed by the cameras' tiny mirrors, too.

The event was widely acknowledged as the "First Swallowing."

Online, people quoted Lovecraft and his works on cosmic horror, drawing parallels between fiction and reality. Eldritch or not, the reflections' reappearance caused an arguably bigger disruption in society than their disappearance. It was one thing to suddenly lose your reflection, and it was another for your reflection to kidnap you.

Most of the time, they behaved as regular reflections, passive and subdued. But when they didn't, it was run or die. Some idiots tried to fight their reflections, but they still disappeared, just into a shattered mirror instead of a smooth one.

Highways and roads around the globe went out of commission. Hundreds and thousands of cars had crashed when the First Swallowing occurred, and the unmanned machines kept piling up. No one was willing to clear out the debris, especially if it meant getting near all that glass.

Theists, especially those of the Abrahamic religions, declared the reflections were "indirect angels" meant to judge humanity and purge sinners. That theory quickly fell apart when the upper echelons of those religions disappeared as they attempted to prove their holiness.

Other spiritualists believed that conquering one's eldritch counterpart was key, so they would host "staring sessions" where people would sit in a room, one mirror each, and stare at their reflection for hours upon hours. Many disappeared, many didn't, but no one knew if the ones who didn't were simply lucky or had developed immunity through their practiced staring. There was no pattern to it. Cryptologists, sociologists, and psychologists huddled together in meeting rooms, scratching their heads over data charts.

Within a week, the world's population decreased by 23 percent. Everyone lost a relative or a friend. It was almost better to have been lonely in the first place. The worst hit were the teens and the middle-aged, who tended to face periods of emotional vulnerability. Those who isolated themselves in their homes drowned in their own paranoia. Some shouted into their mirrors or prayed to whatever god for whatever sign. Some broke the glass in violent fits, and it shattered against their fists, the fragments drilling into their skin, the pain a comforting, lucid proof of existence.

***

On the university campus, the new mirages were an unavoidable curse. It was easy to forget just how many surfaces could act as mirrors when reflections disappeared for a while.

Chloe watched the world keep spinning, holing herself up in the library with her books as a shield. Forget her marketing major, forget Nietzsche; she had returned to the fantasy section, binging several of her childhood favorites each day and constantly discovering more. The world was ending; why not indulge a bit?

Her friends disappeared, one by one. Some were swallowed. Others lost themselves to drugs and returned to haunt the walkways, the smell of weed trailing after them. Yet, it was Chloe who found herself feeling more and more like a ghost. The "normal" person amongst a paranoid, hysterical crowd had become the abnormal one instead.

Chloe still scrolled through social media, now considerably emptier and featuring a lot more pretty flowers and panda cubs tumbling around their playground. Walking back to her dorm, she had memorized a path where to safely direct her eyes, tracing brick and mortar lines, tree shadows, cracks in the cement, and anything not reflective. She had adapted. What else was there to do?

There were others like Chloe, who still tried to maintain a composed air, but not many. They would nod at each other when they crossed paths, strangers united by the common factor of alienation.

Her dorm hadn't changed much, except for all the reflective surfaces being covered with thick black cloth, passed out for free by the government. For now, everyone had to keep their mirrors and glass where they were until the government could coordinate a plan to dispose of an entire nation's worth of mirrors without utterly wrecking the environment. From what Chloe heard, they were looking to establish scientific guidelines and safety protocols before initiating transportation.

She was fine with the status quo for now, but her roommate…

"You're back," a voice rasped from the darkness. Everyone had their own method of feeling safe and Janet's was simply refraining from turning on the lights. If there was no light, there would be no reflection. Problem solved.

It was, in Chloe's opinion, a stupid solution. How was she supposed to live like that? Chloe flipped on the light switch, and the ceiling lamp sputtered to life. Janet shrank further into her bed. She had cocooned herself in a blanket, huddled as she had been for the last two weeks, leaving only her two eyes and an inch of her forehead visible.

"Turn them off," Janet protested in a small voice. "They could come back."

"You're being childish."

Janet didn't answer, so Chloe kept the lights on. She wanted to read, and it's not like she hadn't been triple-checking all the mirror cloaks, at Janet's request, every morning and night.

Janet's condition hadn't been this bad when the reflections first returned. The first week, she tried to keep a sense of normalcy like Chloe, but she was jump scared by a reflection from a spilled pool of water on the bathroom floor and became skittish. Soon, she began to see hallucinations: "mirrors and faces everywhere," she claimed. Now, a month after The First Swallowing, Janet had become her own ghost.

Chloe flopped down on her bed and took out a new book. The concept of studying no longer existed. Her professor was one of the first to be taken, and the college administration had experienced a breakdown in operations and had not yet recovered.

The food delivery guy arrived at 6:30 PM sharp. Chloe grabbed a jacket and trekked outside.

A scrawny man around the same age as her sat on a bicycle at her dormitory gate, holding a plastic takeout bag.

"Thanks." She took the plastic bag from the delivery man, hooking her finger through the tied knot. She caught a whiff of the Chinese takeout inside, still hot and steaming, a welcome contrast to the chilly weather. Her mouth watered as she handed him a ten-dollar bill.

The delivery man didn't hesitate to take the money. "Appreciate it."

Chloe nodded. "How's downtown?"

"Doing alright. People are adapting."

"Yeah?"

"Sort of. There's this trend in my area where people just don't make eye contact with one another, you know, 'cause you can see your reflection in them. Seems like it hasn't caught on with your university yet."

"Huh. That's pretty smart."

"Yeah, but it feels weird, you know? At least things are starting to settle down."

Chloe pursed her lips. "Some of my friends in the city have been talking about a rise in crime."

He shrugged. "There's always been crime. Most people don't want to go outside anymore. It's only the desperate ones who think they have nothing to lose that cause a ruckus."

"Have you been robbed?"

"Not really. I found a way to take advantage of the whole mirror thing. Look." He fumbled in his pouch and took out a covered hand mirror, the kind commonly found in makeup shops. "When someone approaches me menacingly, I'll just take this out and face it in their direction. Scares them off real quick. Kinda like a gun, if you think about it."

"Whoa, I never thought of weaponizing mirrors before. That's pretty genius."

"I know, right?" He smirked.

"You seem to be holding up pretty well despite the apocalypse."

"I mean, an apocalypse ain't taking away the need for food or sleep or a roof over your head. I still gotta make a living." The delivery man smiled, but Chloe could tell it was forced. How many people had he lost? The online death toll was nearing 3 billion, but no census could be truly accurate, given the peculiar state of the global security and communications system.

"You're right. Have a safe trip back."

"Yeah. Thanks, miss."

Chloe returned to her dorm and got out some paper plates, using the chopsticks that came with the takeout bag to eat. As always, she set aside a portion for Janet.

While Chloe's entire marketing career path was circling the drain, Janet's childhood dream of becoming an artist was more than feasible now that animations were the only source of moving picture entertainment and portraits the only way to capture images. Artists could still make it big.

As for Chloe? She was still searching for an alternative path. Maybe she would turn to other business-related majors. Maybe she would try her shot at art. All that time she spent doodling in her notebooks had to count for something. Maybe she would go home first and check on her mother, who has dementia. Oddly, Chloe's future held more possibilities and freedom in the apocalypse. What was her time worth in this new world?

"Chloe."

"Hm?"

Chloe looked up, slightly annoyed at the interruption to her dinner.

"I can't do this anymore," Janet whispered, still huddled in her blanket. "I can't live like this anymore."

"Then don't. Act like you did that first week. You were strong."

"I wasn't."

"I think you were. You're stronger than your reflection. It's just a mirror, no big deal. "

"Don't say that. It gives me chills." Janet shifted, wrapping herself tighter in her cocoon. "Stop talking to me."

Chloe didn't bother to point out the fact that Janet had started the conversation and went back to her dinner.

That night, as she was trying to fall asleep, Chloe could feel Janet's gaze boring into her side. It was a crawling feeling that she had learned to stomach. When Janet first started watching her sleep two weeks before, Chloe turned around to confront her roommate and made a snarky comment. But the eyes that stared back at her held an abyssal quality so unfathomable and empty that Chloe had instantly clamped her lips together and turned back around.

She didn't know when she fell asleep, only that she suddenly jolted awake, feet clammy and hands cold. A noise came from the bathroom. She twisted around to see the bathroom door slightly ajar, light streaming from the crack. Janet wasn't in her bed.

Chloe's heart dropped. From where she lay, she should be seeing the black cover over the bathroom mirror through the door crack. But there was none. Instead, the mirror's naked surface reflected the hand towels on a rack. Chloe edged in closer, careful not to expose herself to the mirror.

Janet's reflection came into view, then her torso. She was leaning against the counter, making direct eye contact with herself, unblinking. What was she doing? Had she finally lost it? Chloe's gaze darted back and forth between Janet and the mirror. Janet's reflection was unmoving as it stared back, very normal, very Janet. It looked even more like the Janet that Chloe knew than the real, physical Janet.

Her roommate raised her hand and pressed it against the glass as if trying to touch the entity on the other side. Her reflection followed.

"Take me," Janet whispered. "Please just take me."

And the mirror answered.

The skin between her hand and the mirror hand merged, the two Janets uniting. Chloe watched the glass swirl, revealing, for the briefest of moments, the abyss that lay beyond its borders. Janet's hand distorted too, followed by her arm and body, sucked into the maws of the gaping void like a drop of bright paint into pitch-black tar. The mirror paused as if digesting its meal, then unswirled, returning to normal display. It did not return Janet.

Half an hour passed before Chloe found the courage to move. She got up from her bed and approached the bathroom, closing her eyes and grasping along the floor until she found the black cloth that Janet had ripped off. She draped it tightly over the mirror.

When she stumbled back into bed, her eyelids felt heavier than ever. Her mind refused to acknowledge the loss. Or maybe it already had; the event processed emotionlessly like any other fragment of information. Maybe, Chloe thought as she drifted off, maybe when she woke up in the morning, the world would've flipped upside down to become right side up again. And if not the next morning, then the morning after that. She will wait for the grief and the relief to come. She will survive to feel it.

Like this, Chloe fell back into a dreamless, unsubstantial sleep.

candidphoto13.jpg

It had been five years since the American branch of the family returned to visit, so the uncles and aunts pooled their money and hired professional photographers to capture the night. Each person was dressed in New Year's clothing even though it was the middle of summer. You could almost smell the fortune through the photo, laced with the aroma of Grandma's mushroom and bamboo shoot soup. The sharp rawness of fresh meat wafted from the kitchen corner where the great-aunts, seated around a round table, were making dumplings with plump pork filling and thin wrappings.

Dinner took place in the basement. The dining table was there, after all. It hadn't moved since it was first placed there thirty years prior, not even when the first floor was built, nor the second, nor the third. Now, the house had five floors, yet the dinner table remained in the basement, surrounded by faded photos on grain shelves and baskets of prepared food hanging from the ceiling to prevent rats from getting into them. There were refrigerators, of course— two in fact, the other was on the fifth floor—but sometimes old solutions worked better.

There was one candid in particular that captured that evening's real energy. On the far left of the photo is a narrow window, almost completely covered in cookware, hung above a small sink. The tiny space beneath the staircase leading up to the garage floor was where all the cooking happened. Water from the pipes, which stubbornly remain leaky after multiple repairs, dripped into a giant bucket that Grandpa would set out at night, collect and dump for the chickens in the morning, and repeat.

The family's two dogs are outside, appearing as underexposed shadows. Their eyes shine, snouts pressing into the mosquito screen door that separates the basement and the courtyard. The courtyard wasn't theirs. It belonged to the neighboring mansion. Derelict and mostly abandoned now, it had been seized by the government during the Communist Revolution and distributed among fourteen poor families, one room each. Great-grandma's family was one of them. Great-grandma herself is nowhere to be seen in the photo, still napping inside the landlord's mansion. She was the only one who continued to live there despite its crumbling infrastructure, in rejection of the new house and all its modern amenities. The family had no argument to convince her to move since she was 96 and in great health.

Grandpa is a blur beyond the kitchen window, bent over the outdoor sink. He's wearing a dark red shirt and a pair of tan, traditional farming trousers. His gray head merges into the evening light. In his hands is a batch of freshly harvested, homegrown vegetables.

On the first floor, the garage floor, more cousins and aunts are arriving, padding down the basement stairs in their Nikes and Crocs. The uncle in the very front, who evidently didn't get the dress code given the Hawaiian shirt he's sporting, extends his arms to no one in particular. Three reuniting sisters follow behind the first uncle, trailed by their children. All of the women had hidden several red packets to be gifted to the youth after dinner. They contained several hundred yuan each, some over a thousand. It was a special occasion—even if they weren't so well off, how could they dare to be stingy tonight?

In the center of all the mayhem is a girl. She looks out of place. While everyone else weaves around her, she sits on an old bench like a lost child at a subway station. She's wearing ripped jeans and a tank top— the only person purposefully not in red. She'd never liked that color, and she grew out of her last set of New Year's clothing eons ago. Her foreign attitude wards off the boisterous anarchy that defines any functional, extended Chinese family.

The girl's father stands next to his older brother, who he hasn't seen in five years. But he's looking at his phone, not his brother, brows furrowed in contemplation. Overseas, he's a successful real estate broker. His beer belly is more prominent than the other men in the room.

The girl's mother hunches over a pot, learning how to make Fu-Jian beef noodles from Grandma. She has an exaggerated yet natural smile on her face, nodding to each syllable the elderly woman says.

The girl's indirect cousins occupy their own hangout spot next to the Moutai shelf. They're playing word games and discussing viral trends on Douyin. The oldest cousin is walking towards the girl with two glasses of plum juice. It wouldn't do to have a guest sit alone. The cousin is a guest himself, coming home after three years away in college in Shanghai. He cuts a tall, wiry figure, earned by late hours hunched over books. He wears square glasses— It would've been strange if he wore none.

The girl's younger cousin, barely in middle school, also wears glasses. With a slumped, begging gesture, he trails after his mother as she navigates the crowded basement to bring a batch of sweet wormwood pancakes—his favorite food—to the kitchen to be diced and arranged. Another plate to add to the table, which is already three-quarters full.

The girl is staring into space. What is she thinking about? With that look on her face, it's as if she's a stranger. Perhaps she feels that way, but even strangers can be family. This feast was organized to celebrate her and her parents' return, after all.

The girl's eyes alight on a familiar, plastic fortune cat perching on a far shelf. It's painted gold, with squinting, smiley eyes.

The cat recognizes her, too. Its raised paw beckons the girl as if saying, "Where in the world were you? It's been so many years. Welcome home."

Made in the USA
Las Vegas, NV
12 December 2024

13943690R00036